P9-DBI-195

JUGGLING

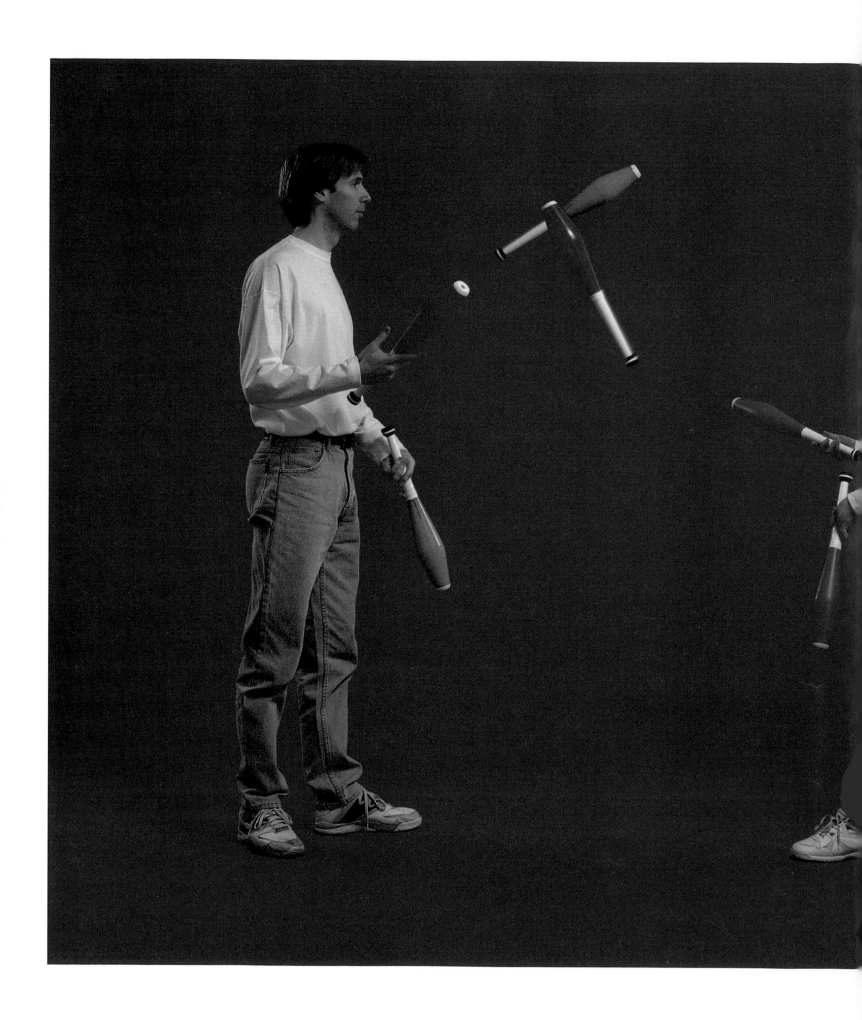

JUGGLING

Charlie Holland

793.87
HOL

Grange
BOOKS

Published Regency House Publishing Limited
The Grange
Grange Yard
London SE1 3AG

Copyright © 1994 Regency House Publishing Limited

Published 1994

All rights reserved. No part of this publication may be
reproduced, stored in a retrieval system, or transmitted
in any form, or by any means, electronic, mechanical,
photocopying, recording or otherwise, without
permission in writing from the publisher.

ISBN 1 85361 408 4

Printed in Italy

Drawings by Ron Brown
Photographs by Michael Plomer

Acknowledgements

The author wishes to thank Katie Norbury for juggling
for the camera, the Oddball Juggling Shop in London
for supplying equipment for the photographs,
everyone at The Circus Space just for being there, and a
special thank you to Caroline Palmer for helping with
the diabolo tricks and everything else. Finally, I would
like to thank Ron Brown and Michael Plomer.

The publishers have made every effort to ensure
that all instructions given in this book are
accurate and safe, but they cannot accept
liability for any resulting injury, damage or loss
to either person or property whether direct or
consequential and howsoever arising.

25.00

CONTENTS

CHAPTER ONE
ANYONE CAN JUGGLE

Why juggle?

The challenge of keeping one more object in the air than we've got hands has fascinated humans since pretty near the beginning of time. After the initial delight of seeming to defeat gravity, however briefly and ungracefully, comes the discovery of how satisfying and soothing the rhythmical nature of juggling is. This is followed by the joy of exploring some of the infinite number of variations possible.

In the same way as you can play music alone, as half of a duo or as a member of an orchestra, so you can juggle alone or with a partner or as part of a group – making music for the eyes.

Finally, unlike most sports, you can juggle almost anywhere and, like music, juggling is a universal language so if you meet a juggler whose language you cannot speak you can at least communicate through juggling together.

What's in the book and how to use it

Chapters One to Three cover ball juggling – starting with the Cascade, the first of the three fundamental juggling patterns, and go on to introduce Columns and the Shower as well as some of the hundreds of variations possible.

Chapter Four introduces juggling with clubs, which you can start to learn as soon as you can juggle the Cascade with balls. Many of the tricks with balls can also be done with clubs.

Chapter Five is about juggling between two or more people. Again you can start to do this shortly after learning the Cascade.

Chapter Six covers skills related to juggling such as the diabolo and plate spinning. You can learn everything in this chapter without being able to juggle at all!

Chapter Seven gives further advice on using juggling in performance. The final chapter is a short history of juggling and jugglers, followed by some useful contacts for more information.

Throughout the text and diagrams work together to explain in detail the progression of every trick while the photographs show tricks in actual performance, their captions often adding extra helpful detail.

The text uses the terms dominant hand and subservient hand. For most people the right hand is the stronger or dominant one. Using the term dominant avoids the complication of confusion for those who happen to be left-handed, or find the left their stronger juggling hand.

When talking about passing, the terms right and left hand have been used instead, because all people involved in a passing pattern have to throw with the same hand – making the right the standard one to use. The onus is on the left-hander to improve his or her right-hand throwing skills

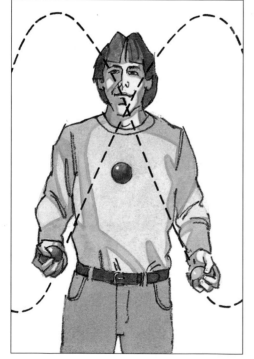

Cascade

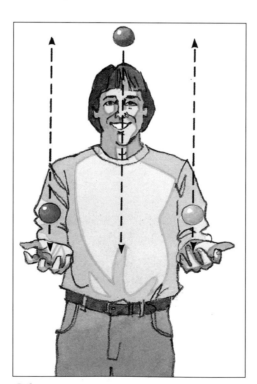

Columns

The Shower

or to find left-handed jugglers to pass with. You may also find that right-handed passers are keen to develop their left-hand passing skills, particularly as many jugglers are now attempting passing patterns involving passing first with the right and then the left hand.

It is a general principle that the more you work on improving your subservient hand the stronger your overall juggling will become. When learning tricks devote an equal amount of time to each hand, or more on your subservient hand. This is of particular importance with moves, such as continuously throwing clubs behind the back, that require you to throw the same trick from your right hand and your left hand.

Learning a trick with your subservient hand forces you to spend more time breaking a trick down into its basic parts. One that comes easily to your dominant hand may require a lot more work with your subservient hand. Attempt to break a trick down into the different steps involved and see whether you can improve the individual steps. Teaching someone else a move is a good way of learning more about it yourself.

It is better to spend several minutes a day on a trick than to spend an hour on one day in the week. If you find yourself getting bored or frustrated try another trick, then come back to the first one. Set yourself challenges and work towards achieving them. Count the number of throws you are doing and try to build up the number you can do without dropping. Do the same for your subservient hand as well as for your dominant one. Work with friends and try to help them in exchange for them helping you. A little friendly competition can motivate both jugglers and lead to improvements. Bear in mind that some people have better eye-hand co-ordination than others. Not everyone will progress at the same pace. The important thing is to perservere and work to achieve the next goal that is appropriate to you, not to someone else.

What to juggle with
You can learn to juggle with just about anything round and reasonably soft, from tennis balls to rolled up socks. You can also buy purpose made juggling bean-bags which are comfortingly squidgy, land firmly in the hand, making them easier to catch, and have the advantage of staying where they land when dropped, rather than rolling under the furniture. Some advice on clubs, diabolos etc. is given in the relevant chapters. Talk to other jugglers and to your local equipment supplier too.

The Cascade

The Cascade is the easiest juggling pattern to learn and the one to which jugglers normally return between tricks. It is the basis for passing balls or clubs too.

The Cascade – starting with one ball
Pick up one ball and throw it from hand to hand. For the Cascade the ball should be thrown with an inward scooping action up to a point just above your head and a little to the other side from the hand which threw it. As you make the throws from right to left hand then left to right hand you can see that the ball is following a figure of eight pattern.

Practise this pattern until the throws are as rhythmical and smooth as possible. The most important rule in juggling is to make your throw as accurate as possible. If the throw is

Throw the ball just above head height so that it peaks on the other side of your body from the hand that threw it.

Throw the ball from hand to hand peaking just above head height.

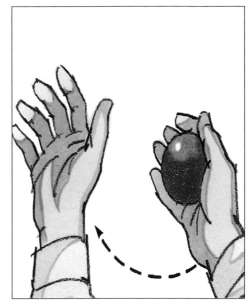

The hand scoops inwards and throws.

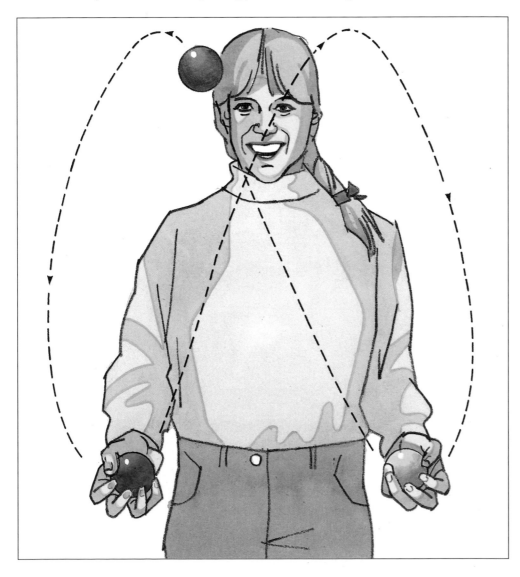

The figure of eight pattern the ball follows.

right the catching will look after itself.

The place to watch is where the ball reaches its highest point. As the ball starts to fall from the peak the mind can compute where and when it will land and move your hand to catch it. You should be catching the ball underhand at about chest height rather than reaching up to grab it.

Look at the illustration of the figure of eight pattern shown on the left. When you are throwing the ball back and forth check that it is going up across your body, because you are making an inward scooping action with your hand (if you make an outward scoop the ball will follow the figure of eight backwards).

Is the ball peaking at the same height when thrown from the left and the right hand? Does the throw from your right hand peak a little to the left of your head, and vice versa?

It is very important in juggling that the throws are consistent. It may help to imagine two points, one either side of your head and a little above it. You can visualise them as a coathanger suspended in the air above and in front of you and aim at its ends. Try to aim the balls to hit those imaginary points when you throw them.

Hold one ball in each hand. Throw the first ball from the dominant hand up and across towards the subordinate hand.

As it peaks throw the ball in the subordinate hand up and across to the dominant hand. It passes below the first ball.

Catch the first ball in your subordinate hand and the second in your dominant hand. Stop. Then throw first from the subordinate hand and then from the dominant one.

Exchanging Two Balls

Throw the balls from one hand to the other as shown in the illustrations. Check that both balls are going to the same height – a little above head height with the ball from your dominant hand hitting an imaginary point above your subordinate hand and then vice-versa.

Initially it can be a good idea to work just on the throwing. Concentrate on getting each ball to hit the imaginary points and let the balls drop to the ground. When you feel you have got it right try it catching them.

Ensure that you are not throwing both balls at the same time by saying throw, throw, catch, catch as you throw and catch the balls.

Make sure that the second ball passes under the first ball.

You may find that your dominant hand is throwing the ball up and across but that your subordinate hand is passing the ball across to the dominant hand. This is probably the way you learnt to juggle two balls at school. To break the habit throw the ball from the subordinate hand first, then the ball from the dominant hand. Aim at the imaginary points mentioned above.

Try to keep the balls in the same plane. If you are throwing the second ball forward this is probably because your mind expects the two balls to collide so it compensates by making you throw one forward. Take a good hard look at the diagram on page 9. The balls do not collide because they are at different points within the figure of eight pattern.

Focus on where the ball peaks. As one ball peaks throw the ball up from the other hand.

Three balls – the complete Cascade

Begin with two balls in your dominant hand and one in your subordinate, as in the photograph below.

Throw the ball held in the fingers of your dominant hand (the red one in the illustration below right) and count 'one'. You always start with the hand that has two balls in it.

When it peaks throw the ball in your subordinate hand, the yellow one, and count 'two'. Catch the red ball. The hand moves outward to receive the ball and inward for the throw.

When the yellow ball peaks throw the remaining, blue, ball from your dominant hand and count 'three' then catch the yellow ball.

When the blue ball peaks throw the ball in your subordinate hand and count 'four'. Keep going – you're juggling.

In reality it is rare to succeed that quickly and easily. Many people find that the third ball gets stuck in their dominant hand and ball two just lands on top of it. Make sure that whatever else happens you throw out the third

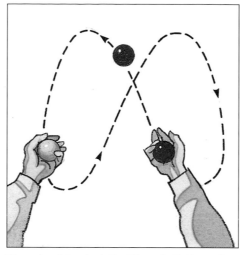

Throw red to start the Three-ball Cascade.

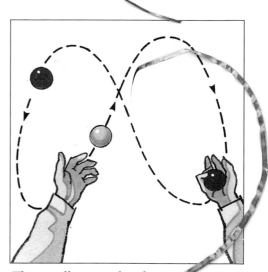

Throw yellow as red peaks.

ball. Try throwing one, two, three without trying to catch at all so you get the rhythm of the throws.

Ensure that the balls arc going to the same height and that you are watching the points where the balls peak. All three balls are following the same figure of eight pattern. They are just at different points within it.

If you find that you are throwing the balls forward try standing with a

wall in front of you and close to it. Try to get the balls to peak a fixed distance from the wall. If they don't they may bounce off the wall making it easier for you can catch them!

If you are getting a sore back from bending down to pick up all the drops try juggling over a bed.

Ask a friend (ideally one who can juggle) to do the trick on the following page with you.

Hold two balls in your dominant hand and one in your subservient hand. The second ball held by the fingers in the hand. This ball will be thrown first.

The yellow ball is about to be thrown. Note how far down the ball has been scooped in preparation for being thrown.

11

Three Balls Between Two People

Standing side by side, one person acts as the right hand and the other as the left hand. Tuck your inside hands behind your backs and use your outside hands to juggle with. This means each person only has to concentrate on one half of the juggle which should make life easier.

Juggle exactly as you would if you were one person. If you experience problems build up to three balls in stages. First throw one ball back and forth. When that is smooth throw two back and forth.

Concentrate as always on making your throws accurate. This lets your partner concentrate on making their throws accurate, which makes catching easier for you!

If one juggler is taller than the other then the shorter juggler may have to throw higher than usual and vice-versa.

After a while change positions so that each juggler gets to experience what it is like being the other hand.

Reverse Cascade
In the standard Cascade you make an inward scoop and throw the ball up through the centre of the figure of eight.

Cascading three balls between two people allows the weaker juggler to concentrate on just one half of the pattern.

Stand side by side with one hand tucked behind the back.

The juggler holding two balls first throws the red up and across.

As the ball peaks the second juggler throws his or her ball and catches the red.

With the Reverse Cascade you make an outward scoop and throw the ball overhand so that it falls through the centre of the figure of eight.

Try this with one ball first. Then take one ball in each hand and throw the first as above. When it peaks throw the second up and over it. The balls should have exchanged hands.

Try this again, starting this time with the ball in the other hand.

Now try with three balls, starting as always with the hand that has two balls in it.

If one hand does the Cascade, making an inward scooping action, and the other does the Reverse Cascade, making an outward scooping action, you create a move called the Half-Shower with the balls from one hand always arcing over the balls being thrown from the other hand. As before, throw each ball as the previous one peaks. Learn this with both hands before trying the next trick

Juggle the Cascade then throw one ball over the top as in the Reverse Cascade. When it lands in the other hand bring that hand out a little to widen the span and throw the ball back over the top again using the Reverse Cascade throw by a stretch of the imagination the sun rising and setting.

It is more impressive if the ball being thrown over the top is a different colour from the other two.

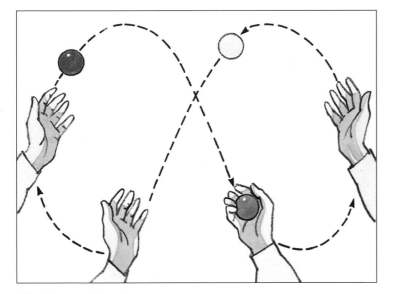

The Reverse Cascade

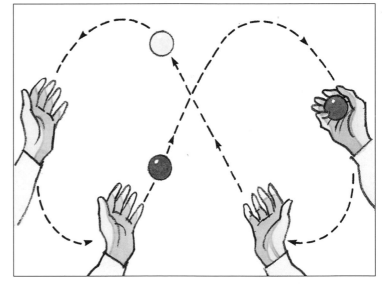

The Standard Cascade

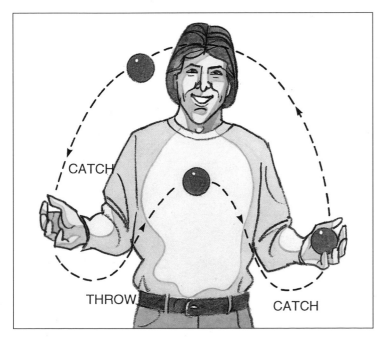

The Half-Shower

Sun Rising and Setting

13

CHAPTER TWO
BEYOND THE CASCADE

In this chapter we develop variations on the Cascade, particularly moves that involve more of the body than just the arms, and learn the other two primary juggling patterns: Columns and the Shower.

Under the Leg

There are four different options for throwing a ball under the leg depending on which leg you throw it under and whether you throw the ball from the outside or the inside of the leg.

Take just one ball and, lifting the right leg, throw it from your right hand under the leg and catch it in your left hand. Next throw the ball from the left hand under the left leg and catch it in the right hand. Now lift your left leg and throw the ball from the right hand under that leg to the left hand. Finally, throw the ball from the left hand under the right leg and catch it in your right hand.

Holding a ball in each hand, raise a leg and throw one ball under before lowering it, throw the second across the body as usual, so that you end up with each ball in the opposite hand.

Take the third ball and, starting with two balls in your dominant hand, raise a leg and start the juggle by throwing the first ball under the leg. Lower the leg and continue to juggle normally.

Now you are ready to try throwing a ball under the leg mid-juggle. With most tricks involving the body it helps to gain some time by giving a little extra height to the ball you throw before you do the main move. So, if you are going to throw the ball from the right hand under a leg, throw the previous ball from the left hand a little higher and vice-versa. See if you can get the same ball to go under the right leg from the outside then under the left leg from the outside then under the right leg from the inside then under the left leg from the inside.

RIGHT
Having thrown the yellow ball up the pink ball will be thrown to make room to catch the yellow. The blue ball will be caught in the right hand.

FAR LEFT
Start the juggle by throwing the first ball under the leg.

LEFT
Give a little extra height to the ball you throw before throwing one under the leg.

14

Behind the Back

Hold one ball in each hand. Throw one up behind your back so that it comes up and around the other shoulder. As it comes into view throw the second ball across your body as usual and catch the first ball.

To learn with three, start with two balls in the subordinate hand.

Throw the first, yellow, up higher than usual. While it is in the air throw

Having released the pink ball behind the back, the right hand is coming back to catch the yellow ball at the front. The blue ball will be thrown out from the left hand to make way for the pink one.

The yellow ball is thrown high from the front, then the red ball from behind.

The yellow ball is caught just before the blue is thrown.

the one in the dominant hand, red, up behind the back.

Bring your dominant hand to the front to catch the yellow ball, then throw the third, blue, and try to keep the Cascade going, repeating the sequence by throwing the red high.

Ensure you work on being able to throw behind the back with your subordinate hand too. When you are competent with each hand see if you can make every throw behind the back. These are called Back Crosses.

Juggling with an arm behind the back
With one ball in your subordinate hand, put your dominant hand with two balls in it behind your back and see if you can juggle keeping it there. If you can, see if you can get back to juggling normally by carrying one of the balls round to the front mid-juggle.

Can you do the same on the other side of your body?

Juggling with an arm behind the back. Each of the balls follows the same sequence.

The Neck Catch

Work with only one ball at first. Throw it straight up in front of you then duck your head and try to catch the ball in the nape of your neck. Keep your head up and your arms outstretched so that you provide a hollow for the ball. Use a bob of the head with an upward jerk of the shoulders to flick the ball back out just before you stand up.

With three balls, Cascade then instead of throwing one of the balls to the other hand throw it straight up so that you can catch it in your neck while holding one ball in each of your hands.

See if you can catch in your neck and flick out every left and right hand throw.

A variation on flicking the ball back into the pattern is to let the ball run down your back, put a hand between your legs and try to catch it.

The neck catch makes an impressive end to a routine.

Spreading your arms wide and tilting your head back allows the ball to nestle in between your shoulder blades.

Throw the ball straight up.

Bend forwards to catch the ball in the neck.

Jerk your head and shoulders to flick the ball into the air.

While the neck catch is a good trick to end a routine, the One Hand Start is a great opening one.

Hold all three balls in your dominant hand. Place two in the palm, held between your little finger and your thumb. The third ball nestles in the other three fingers. Throw all three up and the ball that was in the fingers should separate from the other two and go higher.

With your dominant hand grab the nearest ball, then catch the other lower ball in the subordinate hand. Throw the ball you have just caught in the dominant hand to start the Cascade and catch the last ball.

LEFT
As the balls are released the blue one at the front of the hand rises higher.

The correct position for beginning the One Hand Start.

Once you have mastered the One Hand Start try it under a leg or behind your back.

Grab the nearest then catch the other lower ball in the other hand.

Columns

With Columns the balls go straight up and down parallel with each other rather than crossing as they do in the Cascade. To succeed with Columns you need to be able to juggle two balls in one hand. There are three ways you can do this – as a Column, with an Inward Scoop, and with an Outward Scoop. Try all three ensuring you throw the second ball up as the first peaks.

It is particularly important to spend time developing your subordinate hand also, because for a number of Columns variations you change from doing two in one hand to two in the other. For these tricks to look good both hands need to be equally adept.

Column

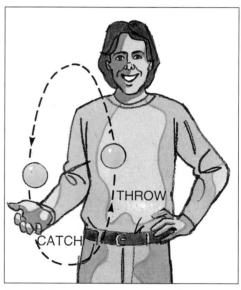

Inward Scoop

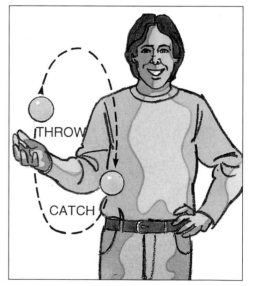

Outward Scoop

The right hand is throwing two balls in one hand in column while the left hand throws one ball up and down.

19

With Columns one ball (the blue one in the illustration) goes straight up and then the other two (yellow) go up parallel to each other.

Begin by holding two balls in your dominant hand, one in your subordinate one. Throw the first, the blue ball from the dominant hand, straight up centrally. When it peaks throw the other two, yellow, balls straight up at the same time on either side of the first ball. Catch the blue ball and throw it straight back up the middle, then catch the other two and throw them straight back up either side. Experiment catching the blue ball alternately in the right and left hand.

Now you can move the individual ball around the two other balls which, for the tricks to look effective, should continue to go up and down in exactly the same place and should peak at exactly the same height.

Throw the blue ball from the right hand up to your right then throw the yellow two up normally.

Take the hand out to catch the blue. The other hand throwing before the catch.

As the yellow balls peak and start to descend the blue one will be thrown straight up.

20

Move your right hand in to throw the blue ball up the middle and catch the yellow balls.

Catch the blue ball in the left hand on its descent and move your hand to the left.

Throw the blue ball up on the left hand side and catch the yellow balls.

Missing out the middle move

Throw the blue ball up to your right side then throw the two yellow balls up. When the blue ball comes down catch it in your right hand and immediately pass it to your left hand and throw it up to the left before catching the two yellow balls.

Throwing two over the one

Instead of throwing the blue ball up the middle and then the two yellow balls up parallel to each other, you can throw the yellow ones up so that they either cross over or hit each other and bounce back.

Missing out the middle move.

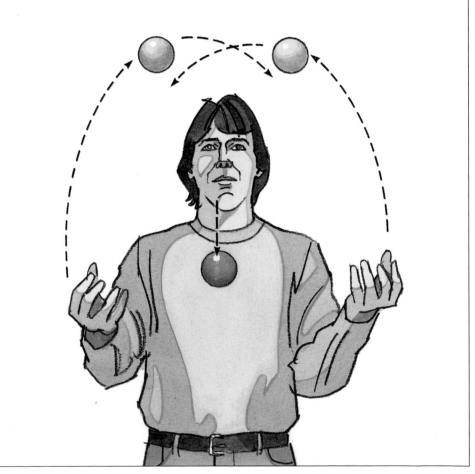

Throwing two over the one.

The Cheat

This is exactly the same as Columns except that instead of throwing both yellow balls up you carry one of them up and down. Juggle two balls in Columns in your dominant hand. Hold the third ball in the fingertips of your subordinate hand so that most of the ball is visible to an onlooker. As you throw the outside ball of the Columns up mirror that ball's movements with your subordinate hand. It takes several moments for an audience to realise that you are cheating.

Work on getting the cheat ball to stop at the same height as the thrown ball. Try making very small Columns and Columns so tall that you have to stand on tip-toe to reach with the Cheat.

The left hand holding one yellow ball mirrors the movement made by the other yellow ball.

The Cheat

The Yo-Yo

This is a variation on The Cheat where the cheat ball is moved up and down on top of the inside ball of the Columns to look as though the two balls are attached by invisible string.

If you move the cheat ball up and down *under* the inside ball you are doing the Oy-Oy, or Australian Yo-Yo.

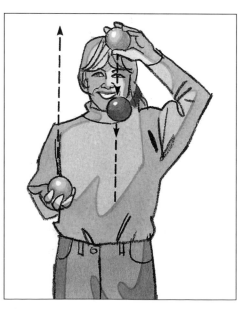

The Yo-Yo

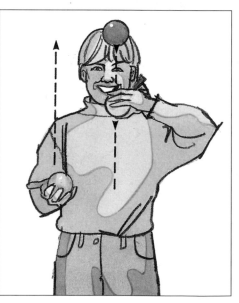

The Oy-Oy

22

The right hand is throwing one yellow and one blue ball up in columns. The other yellow ball is moved up and down above the blue ball so that they seem to be attached by a string.

The Yo-Yo with no Strings

When juggling two balls in one hand there is a moment when one ball is peaking and one is in the hand. At this moment you can take the cheat ball through the middle without interrupting the pattern. Then try to take it back again

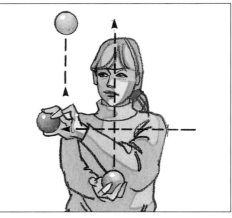

Taking the cheat ball through the middle.

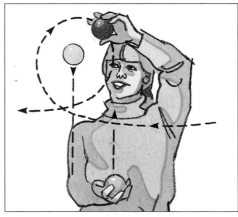

As an alternative carry the cheat ball around the nearest ball as it peaks.

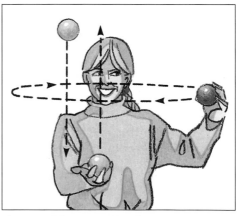

As you pick up speed and accuracy move the cheat ball across and back in one gap.

23

The Shower

In this juggling pattern three balls follow each other in a circle. Hold two balls in your dominant hand and one in your subordinate hand. Then from the dominant hand throw first one ball, then the second very quickly afterwards. The balls make an arc a little above head height aiming to arrive in your subordinate hand.

While the two balls are in the air you half pass and half throw the ball in your subordinate hand to your dominant hand. As soon as a ball arrives in the dominant hand you must throw it out in the arc again.

Two balls in the dominant hand to start.

As two balls are up in the air the left hand slides a ball across to the right.

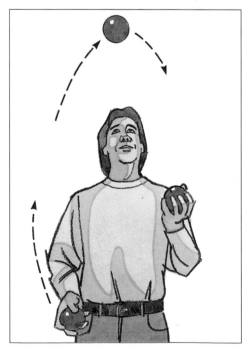

Throw balls in quick succession.

Pass the third ball.

Throw the passed ball immediately.

24

The Giraffe

Hold your subordinate hand up high and taking just one ball throw it up from the dominant hand so that it lands accurately in the subordinate hand. Then tip the ball out of the hand and catch it in your dominant hand again. Practise this until you hardly have to move the subordinate hand to catch and throw the ball.

Next, hold one ball in each hand and, as the ball thrown from the dominant hand is about to land in the subordinate hand, tip the ball held in it out.

Finally, hold two balls in your subordinate hand and one in your dominant hand. Tip a ball out from the subordinate, top hand and before it lands throw the ball in the dominant hand up. Before that one lands tip the third ball out and repeat the pattern.

Drop the ball in the palm of the top hand down; throw the ball in the lower hand up.

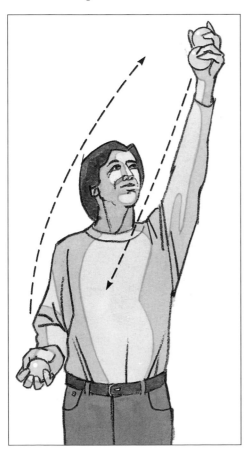

The Giraffe.

The right hand is about to catch the lower ball. The middle ball is going up to the left hand. Just before the middle ball is caught the top ball will be dropped.

CHAPTER THREE
ADVANCED BALL JUGGLING

In this chapter we tackle some of the harder ball tricks plus juggling four and five balls. Don't be afraid to skip this chapter for the moment if you would rather learn to juggle clubs or get to grips with the diabolo first.

Clawing and releasing one ball catching and throwing the ball from on top.

Take one ball and instead of holding it on your hand turn your hand upside down so your hand is gripping the ball from above. Keeping your hand on top throw the ball out by raising your hand giving a bit of a wrist flick. Then raise your other hand to catch the ball by making an action like a cat clawing, so that you are catching it from on top. Practise this and see how fast and furious you can make the action.

Juggle three balls and learn to claw with just one hand, then learn with the other hand. Finally try to claw with both hands as in the photograph on the left. You may find it helps to leave out the third ball initially and practise with just two balls clawing both of them.

See how small and frantic you can make the pattern and then how big and languid.

The right hand is about to snatch the ball while the left hand is about to throw the ball up.

26

Bouncing five balls.

The Penguin

The Penguin is a difficult move based on catching the balls when your hands are twisted around. We'll get on to why it's called the Penguin in a moment.

First practice the movement using only one ball. Hold your left hand as though about to catch normally and then twist your arm and wrist clockwise. Straighten your arm and keep it tucked in close to your body. Throw a ball from your right hand across your body and catch it in your twisted left hand. Then untwist the left hand to throw normally, while twisting the right hand to throw the ball.

Now try using two balls with a ball in each, twisting both hands outwards.

Untwist one hand and throw the ball then immediately twist the hand back again. As the ball peaks untwist the other hand, throw the second ball and twist the hand back to catch the first ball. Finally, catch the second ball in the twisted first hand.

Throw from your right hand to your twisted left hand.

For the best effect keep the arm straight by your side when catching a ball in it.

Untwist one hand to throw the ball, follow with the other hand as it peaks, twisting back after the throw, ready for the next catch.

28

Untwist your left hand so that you can throw normally.

Twist your right hand to catch the ball.

Two balls: holding one ball in each hand, twist both hands away from the usual position.

The full Penguin juggles three balls, always catching twisted.

Both hands twist in to throw and back out again to catch the next ball.

Half a Penguin

When your performance with two balls is fairly smooth add a third: two in your dominant hand as normal and one in your subordinate hand which is twisted. Throw and catch balls in the dominant hand as normal but try to catch every ball in the subordinate hand with it twisted, then untwist and throw.

Try the same with the dominant hand twisted and the subordinate as usual.

The Full Penguin

For the Full Penguin, using three balls, change to have both hands catching twisted, as you did when juggling two balls. The final step in creating the Penguin is to stand with your legs together and feet turned out. As you juggle catching the balls with your hands outturned and your arms rigidly by your side you are starting to look like a penguin. To complete the image try to waddle forward at the same time.

Mills Mess

This is a very difficult trick which makes jugglers very satisfied when they finally learn it. Naturally enough they show it off to an onlooker to whom it looks a complete mess! It's not an easy trick to learn just from a book so try to find a juggler who can do Mills Mess to help you.

Follow the moves in the illustration sequence, with one ball in your dominant hand.

Now reverse the move by throwing the ball from your subordinate hand back towards your subordinate side and uncross and recross your arms so that your dominant hand is on top and catch the ball in it. You are now in the mirror image of where you where when you started, with your subordinate hand instead of your dominant hand on top.

One Ball

Hold a ball in your dominant hand and cross your arms so that your dominant hand is on top. Throw the ball back towards your dominant side.

While the ball is arcing, uncross and recross your arms so that your subordinate hand is on top and ready to catch the ball.

The Mills Mess in action.

Three Balls

Start with three balls, place a second (blue ball) in the dominant hand which is crossed over your subordinate hand. Throw the front two balls as in the two – ball version.

Catch the red ball in your subordinate hand and as your dominant crosses underneath throw the blue ball straight up before catching the yellow ball.

For the first few times just let the blue ball fall to the ground.

The next step is to throw the red ball back from the subordinate hand to the subordinate side and as you uncross the subordinate hand you catch the blue ball in it.

Two Balls

Taking two balls adopt the starting position as with one. Hold a ball (red) in your dominant hand which is crossed over your subordinate hand which is holding another coloured ball (yellow).

RIGHT
Cross your hands so that your subordinate hand is on top and catch the red ball in your subordinate hand while the yellow ball is caught by your dominant hand as you cross it.

Throw the red ball from your dominant hand back across your body to your dominant side and uncross your hands.

Throw the yellow ball from the subordinate hand up as if to follow the red ball, but without travelling so far.

Reverse the move so that you end up with the dominant hand on to the red ball in it.

Keep doing and reversing the move until it becomes smooth. You may be able to spot the gap for the third ball where a hand is crossed under the other.

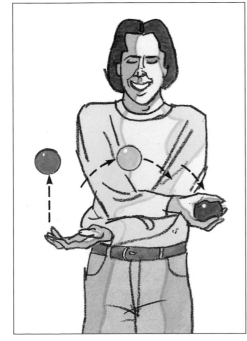

Carry the blue ball under the dominant hand and throw it straight up.

It is caught by the dominant hand and carried under and thrown back up the subordinate side.

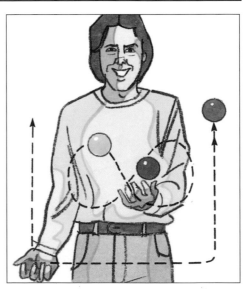

All the blue ball is doing is being thrown up one side and caught, being carried across the other side, thrown up and caught, being carried back and the pattern repeated while the other two balls are exchanged in a tight cascade.

Four Balls

If you can juggle two balls in your subordinate hand in a controlled manner then you can juggle four! The easiest way of juggling four is to simply juggle two in each hand. The balls do not change hands. The same rule, incidentally, applies for any even number of objects, so to juggle six, juggle three in each hand.

Most people find the inward scoop the easiest pattern.

Inward and Outward Scoops

Throw a ball from each hand at the same time with an inward scoop so the balls circle outwards. Check that the balls are going to the same height. As they peak throw the next two up. Try the outward scoop too.

To make juggling four look more complicated throw alternately from each hand rather than at the same time. So you throw right, left, right, left in sequence. You are still juggling two balls in each hand but by throwing from each hand at different times it looks as though the balls are crossing from one hand to the other even though they are not. This effect

Four ball juggling with two being thrown up parallel at the same time.

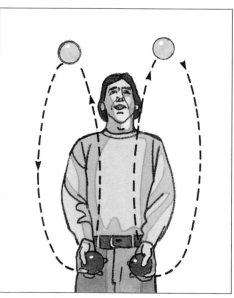

Inward Scoop

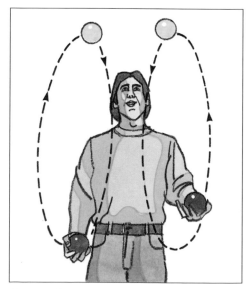

Outward Scoop

is heightened if your balls are two different colours, with one of each in each hand – as shown in the photo on the right.

Juggling four by throwing alternately from each hand.

Splits

A very impressive variation is Splits, when you throw a ball from each hand simultaneously up to your right side in parallel columns and then throw the next two up to your left side. It helps to shift your hips and shoulders from side to side.

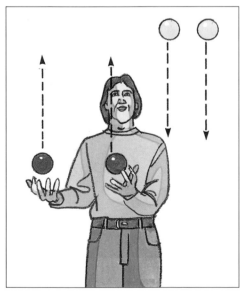

Splits

The staggered four ball pattern with the balls thrown up alternately

33

Five Balls

Juggling five balls is much harder than four and much, much harder than juggling three. The Cascade is the pattern used – and this is the easiest for juggling odd numbers whether three, five or seven objects.

What happens is that you throw the first three up – one from the dominant hand, one from the subordinate, another from the dominant – and while they are in the air you throw the next two up – one from the subordinate hand, one from the dominant.

A Three ball Flash is a good way to start to work up to five. Hold just three as for the normal Cascade and throw them higher and faster than usual. The idea is to get all three of them in the air at the same time. You throw right, left, right then catch left, right, left. While all three are in the air try to clap your hands, as in the

The Five-ball cascade.

photograph below, before catching them again. This helps give an idea of the speed, accuracy and height needed in juggling five.

Also practise holding three in the right hand and throwing them up and across to the left hand quickly – in effect just doing the right hand part of the pattern. The first ball should not arrive in the left hand until the last has left the right hand. Catch all the balls in the left hand then repeat the action towards the right hand. When you have got the hang of this, instead of gathering the balls in the receiving hand throw each one straight back out as it lands so that the three balls follow each other around the pattern in five ball timing.

With five, practise throwing the five up quickly and accurately – right, left, right, left, right without trying to catch them at all to perfect your throw. Imagine there are two targets, one either side of your head and a little higher, and try to hit them

Throw three balls up in the air and clap your hands before catching the balls.

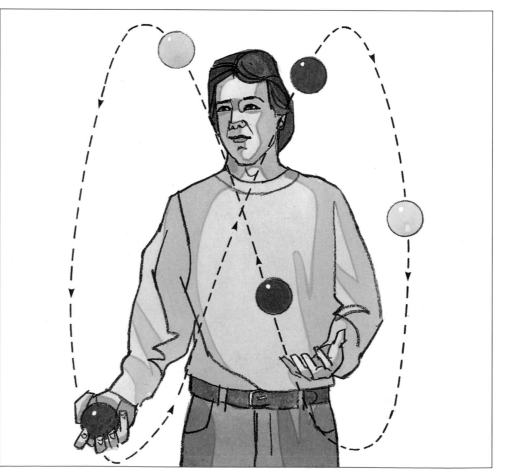

The Five-ball Cascade.

with the balls. After that the performance of this trick is a case of practise, practise, practise trying to get the pattern as controlled and fluid as possible.

Half-Shower with Five Balls

Many of the variations that are possible with three ball juggling can also be done with five balls. An example is the Half-Shower which was covered in chapter one with three balls. The five ball version is exactly the same, with the dominant hand making an outward scooping action and the subordinate handing still doing an inward scooping action.

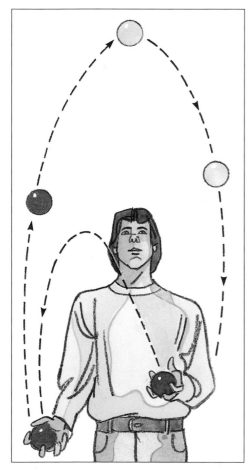

The dominant hand throws balls in an arc over the ball thrown from the subordinate hand. The subordinate hand moves inwards after the catch to make a smaller one.

The Five-ball Half Shower

Ball Bouncing

Bouncing three balls

Ball bouncing offers a myriad of opportunities. The best balls to use are made of silicon and when dropped bounce back to almost the same height. This makes it very easy to scoop them up before allowing them to drop them down again. The ideal surface for bouncing is smooth, level and very hard – for example a marble slab or floor. However ordinary rubber or tennis balls on a gymasium floor are adequate for many tricks.

When bouncing balls you have two main options, depending on whether you force the balls down by keeping your hands palm downwards or whether you throw the balls up a little as in the Reverse Cascade. In the latter case you gain time with the upward throw making it easier.

It is also possible to Shower three balls as shown below.

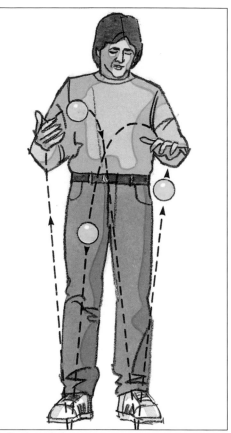

Balls forced down

Force bouncing three balls

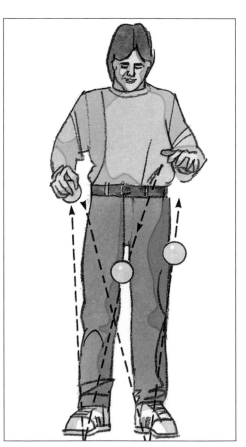

Bounce Reverse Cascade

Bounce Shower

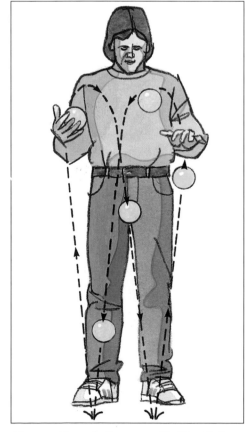

Reverse Cascade Bounce with Five Balls

Bouncing five balls

This is easier than juggling five balls in the air because you are not fighting gravity so much, plus with the reverse cascade bounce you are gaining extra time as you do with three balls. Just as you try to hit imaginary points in the air when throwing balls up so you should try to get the balls to hit the equivalent two points on the ground.

A nonchalant pose makes the trick look even more effective.

CHAPTER FOUR
JUGGLING CLUBS, FIRE TORCHES AND RINGS

Having learnt to juggle balls most people want to advance to the more spectacular clubs, torches and rings. Nearly all tricks that you can do with balls can also be done with clubs or rings.

Throwing a club
The essential difference between juggling clubs as against balls is that the club makes a revolution in the air which has to be controlled. The clubs are weighted so that they spin when thrown. They are difficult to throw without them doing so. The stronger the throw the greater the number of spins it will produce.

Practise tossing the club up and down in one hand so that it makes one revolution before you catch it. Hold the club so that it is parallel to the ground then lower your arm and throw the club up, using more arm than wrist movement. See also if you can make a double spin by throwing with a little more force.

Next practise throwing a club from one hand to the other as described below. Try using one club and two balls in a cascade pattern to get the rhythm of juggling.

Fire juggling – very difficult in absolute darkness as you can see the flame but not the handles!

Club Juggling

There are many types of clubs on sale at juggling shops and you should ask them for advice on which to buy. To a large extent it is a matter of personal preference. However, if you have a local juggling group I advise you to choose a similar club to those used in the accompanying photographs and drawings as it is easier to pass with other people if your clubs are a similar weight, shape and length to theirs. Light and slim clubs are better for numbers juggling (that is juggling four or five) and are easier to catch the wrong way round – something that often happens when learning! For juggling outdoors a heavier club is better as it is not blown off course in the breeze. Bear in mind that for performing purposes, clubs with fat bulbs are more visible.

Practise throwing the club from one hand to the other. Start with the club held out at about 45° from your side.

Practice a Cascade with balls and one club.

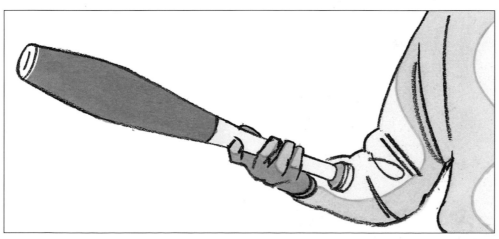

A Club is designed to be thrown from the middle of the handle. If you hold it by the knob and throw it you are likely to hit yourself in the face.

Lower your arm down and then scoop up, throwing the club as it becomes parallel with the ground. Catch it in your other hand.

Holding clubs ready to start.

Juggling three clubs

Firstly take one club in each hand and practise exchanging them, throwing the club from your dominant hand and as it turns throwing the club in the subordinate hand.

To juggle three clubs, hold two in your dominant hand as shown in the photograph. The pink club will be thrown first.

To stop juggling catch a club in your dominant hand, the second in your subordinate hand and as the final one comes toward your dominant hand ensure the first club is gripped by the thumb so you can stretch out your fingers to clasp the third club.

You can practise throwing the occasional club with a double instead of a triple spin. Alternatively throw every club with a double, or by throwing it a little more forcefully, a triple spin. See how high and slow you can make the double spin and also

Having thrown the orange club the right hand can now catch the green one.

Scoop and throw the first from the hand holding two.

When the first club turns scoop and throw the second. Catch the first.

As the second club turns scoop and throw the third. When that turns throw the first club, which will now be in the opposite hand.

40

how low and fast you can make it. Try with triple spins as well.

Run through the moves that you can do with three balls, such as under the leg, and try them with clubs. You may find it helps to attempt the trick with just one club or one club and two balls first.

Kick-Up

An impressive way of starting or of picking up when you have dropped its to kick the club up.

Place the club on your foot with the body of the club towards the outside and angled towards the front. Keep you toes lifted so that the handle is on your foot and the club nestles between the top of your toes and your shin. Keep your foot flexed as you kick backwards and up. The handle catches your shin and the club makes a single spin to your hand.

You may be able to drop a club while juggling so that it lands on the foot and can be kicked straight back up into the pattern. This looks very good when clubs are dropped either side so it is worth while learning to kick up with either foot.

The kick up is also useful when passing clubs as a way of recovering from a drop. as well as kicking up to yourself kick up direct to your partner instead of throwing a club across.

Kick the red club and throw the right hand club up so that you can catch the red.

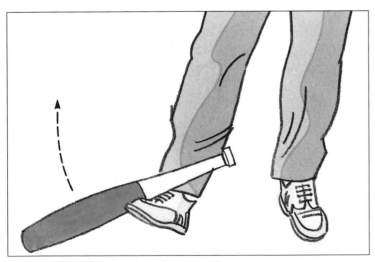

Start position for the Kick-Up.

Bring the foot backwards and up.

41

Chops

In this impressive but difficult move you are continuously bringing clubs in the hand in a chopping action down and across the body. You may find it helps to learn this with balls first. Start with just one club in each hand.

Chop one club down, throw the second underneath and throw the first club up.

Lift the one in the dominant hand up and chop it across your body, as if chopping wood. Throw the club in the subordinate hand under the dominant hand as shown in the illustration on the left. Throw the club from the dominant hand at the bottom of the chop. At this point your arms are crossed. Uncross you arms and catch the first club thrown in your dominant hand. Catch the second club in the subordinate hand. Repeat this until it is a smooth action.

Now learn the same move with the subordinate hand making the chopping action. Finally alternate chopping with the dominant hand then chopping with the subordinate.

With three clubs learn first how to chop with just the dominant hand: start with two clubs in the subordinate hand. Chop the dominant hand across and throw the first club in the subordinate hand under the dominant hand. Throw the second club from the dominant hand as previously. Catch the first club in the dominant hand, chop down and throw the third club under the dominant hand. Catch the second club in the subordinate hand. You should now be continuously chopping with the dominant hand and continuously throwing under it with the subordinate hand.

Learn the same move with the subordinate hand chopping instead of the dominant hand.

To chop alternately with the right and left hand begin in the same way and then follow the illustrations below.

The left hand is about to chop the pink club down across the body.

Reach up with the subordinate hand to catch the orange club and chop it down as you throw the pink club up to your subordinate side.

Chop the pink club in the dominant hand down and across your body while throwing the green club underneath.

Catch the green club and chop it down then throw it up as you chop the pink club down over it.

42

Behind the Back

Take one club and throw it up behind your back so that it comes round your shoulder and can be caught in practically the same position as you would catch a normal throw. Ensure that you are turning your head and are giving the club enough height to be able to spot it. Try with a double spin too, which give you more time.

Juggle three clubs as normal and try to throw one behind you back. To gain some time it helps to give the previous club a little extra height. Experiment with a double spin again. Build up from throwing an occasional club behind the back to every throw with one hand.

Make sure that you practise with both hands. When you are competent with each hand try Back Crosses – where every throw is made behind the back. Accuracy is paramount with Back Crosses. Try to avoid throwing clubs wide or too low. Double spins are easier than singles because each club is longer in the air, giving you more time to react.

Having released the orange club behind the back the right hand will return to catch the green one.

For Back Crosses, throw a club behind the back.

As it peaks throw the club in the other hand behind the back. Repeat with each.

The Club Balance

Learn to balance one club on another as shown in the photograph. You need to focus on the top of the club being balanced. If it tilts forward you must push the club beneath forward to compensate. By pushing a bit further forward the club on top will tilt back, allowing you to bring your hand back.

At first you will need to move your hand a lot, but gradually you will be able to spot a tilt beginning and take rapid action to correct it. Ultimately you hardly move your hand at all.

While juggling, throw the club in your dominant hand straight up with a double spin. While that club is in the air catch the next club to arrive in the dominant hand and place it onto the club in the subordinate hand. Catch the club you threw with a double spin in your dominant hand.

Use the club in your hand to flick the balanced club off to start juggling again.

A variation is to see if you can flick the club being balanced over and catch its bulbous end in the same place.

One club can be balanced on the other.

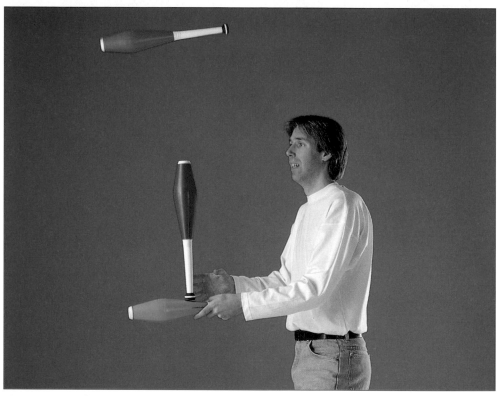

Concentrate on keeping the club balanced rather than on catching the club down to the right hand.

Fire juggling is as effective from the side.

If you can't juggle clubs without catching the right end everytime then you aren't ready to juggle fire.

Juggling Fire Torches

Have you ever wondered where the expression "a sure-fire crowd pleaser" came from? It may not have come from fire juggling but there's no doubt that fire juggling is a mesmeric and amazing spectacle.

As with all other activities involving fire it can be dangerous and should be done only outdoors with no combustible materials nearby and with someone on hand with a fire extinguisher should something go wrong.

If you decide to juggle fire ensure that you use well made fire torches from a reputable dealer and keep them well maintained. Ask the dealer's advice about which low volatile fuel to use, e.g. kerosene (paraffin) or white spirit. **Never** use petrol or gasoline. Keep the fuel in a fireproof and sealable container.

Dip the wicks completely for two or three seconds and then vigorously shake off excess fuel to avoid sparks flying off. Practise juggling the torches unlit first. Remember that after they have been lit the drag caused by the flame will make them rotate more slowly. Before lighting the torches check that the wind is blowing away from you.

If a club lands with the burning end in your hand you will drop it very quickly and it is unlikely to burn you.

The yellow ring starts to fall, the red ring will be thrown up.

The starting position with three rings. The yellow ring is held by the thumb and forefinger.

Rings are excellent for number juggling as they are so narrow that there is little risk of collision when they are in the air. However it is hopeless to try to juggle with them when there is any wind. Give each ring a spin as you throw it up otherwise they wobble.

One of the nicest effects with rings is the colour change– done with one hand or, for added speed with both. Buy rings which have a different colour on each side or stick two rings together (use double sided tape if you want to separate them later!).

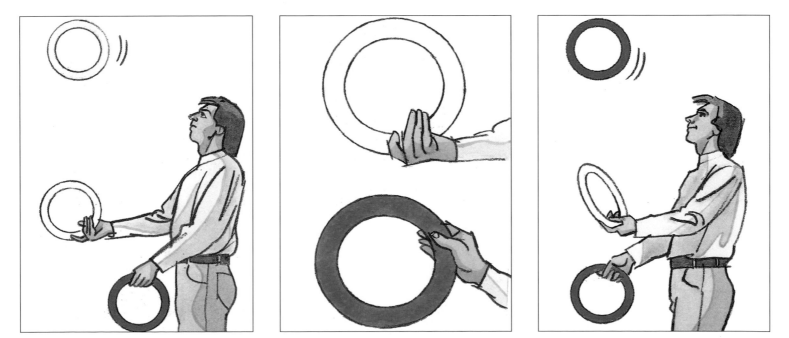

To make a ring change colour in front of the audience's eyes, catch it underhand, turn and throw.

From working with one other person to working with the equivalent of an orchestra there is endless scope for exploring manipulative juggling patterns.

This chapter looks at a couple of variations on juggling three objects between two people then moves on to passing balls and clubs. Many of the tricks previously covered in the book can be incorporated into passing with a little experimentation.

As soon as you have the Cascade mastered try to get together with other jugglers and develop the skills needed to pass. Details of how to get in contact with other jugglers are given at the end of the book.

Most jugglers relish the opportunity to get together with one or more other jugglers and hurl objects around. One of the great things about juggling is the mutual dependence that makes co-operation essential. With passing it is particularly important to try to make your throws as catchable as possible. Determine where you need to throw to for your partner to make any easy catch and aim at that point. Share time with people you are passing to – equally if you've had five goes at getting a trick right let them have five goes at a trick.

If you are lucky an experienced juggler will give you some time to help you develop. When you have become a proficient passer and a beginner comes along please give them some of your time and help.

Passing six clubs between two people.

46

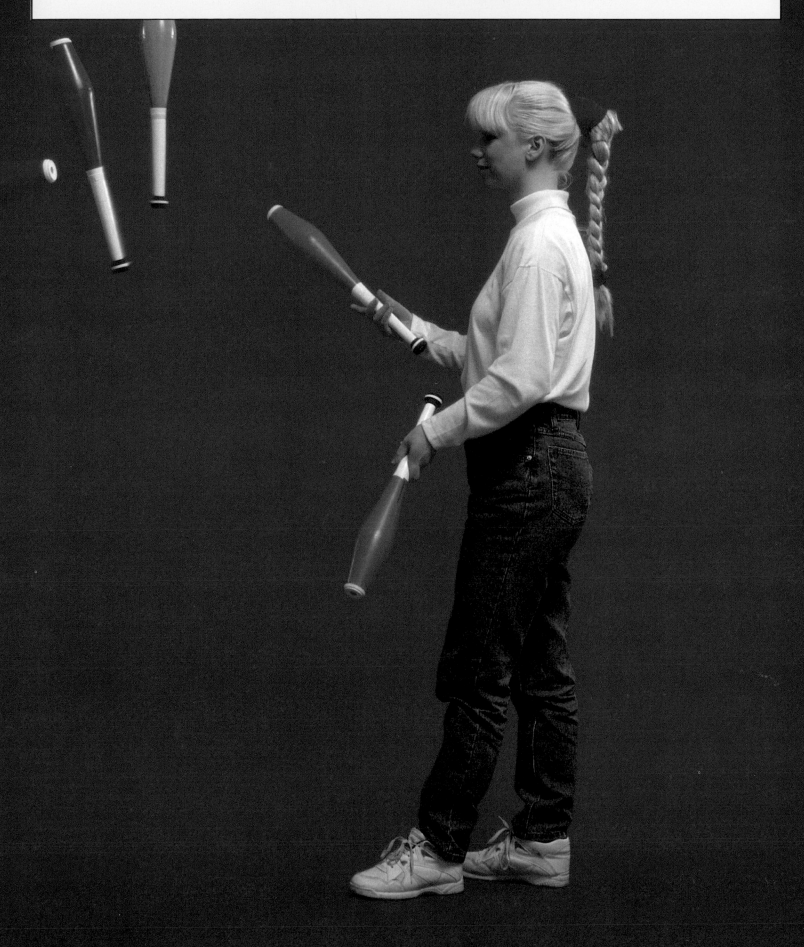

CHAPTER FIVE
JUGGLING ALONG WITH OTHER PEOPLE

Stealing from the side.

Stealing

Stealing from the front
In this trick a fellow juggler cascades three balls facing you. You reach out and steal all three without breaking the pattern. Your fellow juggler should help you steal the balls by juggling slowly, throwing the balls a little higher than usual. Initially it may help if the balls are thrown slightly towards you. However this looks less real to an audience.

Practise stealing the balls backwards and forwards between each other. See if you can take the balls straight back off each other without a pause. A variation is to steal just one ball. Your partner continues to juggle as normal with a gap where the stolen ball would be. Find the moment where the stolen ball would peak and drop it back into the pattern.

As your partner, mid-juggle, throws up a ball from the left hand you steal it with your left hand as it peaks.

As the next ball peaks, coming out of your partner's right hand, you steal that in your right hand. You now have one ball in each hand.

As your partner's third ball peaks you throw the one in your right hand in the regular Cascade and catch the third ball. You are now juggling all three.

Stealing from the side
Stand to the left of your partner who is juggling normally. Slide your right hand across your partner's chest, though you will steal the first ball with your left hand. Take the second ball with your hand and incorporate the motion of the third into your own juggling. While you juggle, your partner can now step to the right and come around you to your left to steal the balls of you. As you become more proficient you can speed up the stealing so that it seems as though the balls stay in one place with the two jugglers making ever faster circles. This is known as the run-around and is also looks very good with clubs.

With your left hand reach in and steal the ball thrown from your partner's right hand as it peaks.

Your right hand is in place to take the next ball as it goes towards your partner's right hand.

You now have one ball in each hand. The third ball thrown by your partner becomes the first ball in your juggling pattern.

Passing six balls between two jugglers

A pre-requisite for successfully passing balls is being able to juggle smoothly and consistently while looking through the pattern at something or someone else. Instead of concentrating on your pattern you need to be able to focus on the point to which you want to throw, and that from which a ball will be thrown to you.

You also need to make sure that you are juggling at the same tempo as your partner – neither faster nor slower – and to the same height. This allows you to throw the balls out at the same moment.

Stand facing your partner as a distance of about six feet (1.8 m). There is a standard procedure to ensure that you start juggling together. Each juggler holds his or her hands raised with two balls in the right and one in the left hand. One is the leader and will say 'Go' at which point you both lower your hands and start juggling, without passing, but synchronising your throws.

Practise this, counting each throw you make from your right hand out loud. If you are not counting at the same time you are out of sychronisation. Try to alter your juggling speed or height to match your partner's timing.

Holding the balls ready to start

Give the balls a gentle lob to your partner rather than throwing them across.

To learn passing it is easiest to learn with five balls – you have three balls and your partner has two, one in each hand.

Start as described above but only you juggle. Your partner makes room for the ball being thrown to him or her by throwing the ball in the left hand out to begin juggling. Initially every fourth throw from the right hand will be thrown across. Rather than counting One, Two, Three, Four do a countdown as follows: Three, Two, One, Pass.

Throw the ball directly across in a gentle lob from your right hand to your partner's left hand. As it comes in he or she throws the ball in the left hand out to begin juggling normally. Your partner counts down with every right hand throw he or she makes and the fourth throw is towards your left hand.

When throwing to a partner it is important to concentrate on making it as accurate and easy to catch as possible. Look at the point where you want the ball to land rather than just throwing the ball in the general direction.

When you are confident with five move on to six, so that you are juggling and passing at the same time as each other. Try passing every third ball from the right hand (known as passing on thirds), then every second (passing every other) and finally every one (showering).

Remember:
SHOWERING is passing every ball, PASSING EVERY OTHER is passing every second ball, and THIRDS is passing every third

3-3-10

3-3-10 is a standard pattern which works very well in front of an audience as the rate of passing gets faster and faster. It comprises three thirds (two, one, pass), three every others (one, pass, one, pass) and ten showers (pass, pass, pass, pass, pass, pass, pass, pass, pass, pass)

The Slow Start and The Fast Start

There is a standard slow start which is to bring your hands down on 'Go' and do two self throws from the right hand and pass the third across. So, for example, a 'slow start: shower' is counted 'Go, two, one, pass, pass, pass, ...'

With the fast start you bring your hands down on 'Go' and immediately start to pass. So, a 'fast start: every others' is counted 'Go, pass, one, pass, one, pass, one, pass....' and so on.

Recovering drops when passing

You needn't stop juggling when you drop a ball. Juggle on thirds and drop a ball on purpose near your right foot. Stop juggling, holding one ball in each hand until your partner throws the normal pass across to you. You then juggle, and your partner stops. On usual thirds timing pass the ball across to him or her and immediately bend down to pick up the dropped ball with your right hand. Throw it across at the same time as your partner throws to you on thirds timing and you will both be juggling again.

The same principle holds true on every others; you just have less time to make the pick up. On a shower there will be a gap being passed around the pattern where the dropped ball normally is. When the gap comes to your right hand you must pick up and throw the dropped ball in one rapid, smooth action.

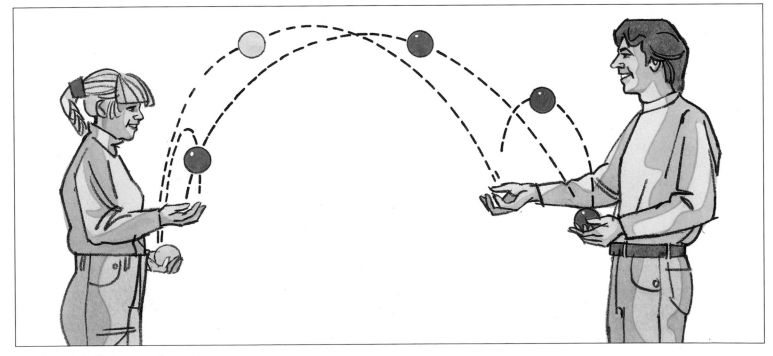

Passing six balls in a regular pattern.

Passing Clubs

The fundamentals of passing clubs are the same as those for passing balls with the addition of the spin. The club should make a single revolution between you and your partner. It should be aimed at a point just to his or her left at about shoulder height.

It helps it you stand with your right leg slightly back. The club you are going to pass should be swept back by your right leg before being thrown. This should ensure that there is sufficient arm movement rather than too much wrist action which results in a short, fast spin.

It is very important that each juggler concentrates on the accuracy of their throws. There's little worse than having a club hurtling directly towards your face!

Learn on thirds timing, then work towards every others and showering.

Double and Triple Spins
These, and many other tricks, are best learnt on every other timing.

A double spin is when a club makes two revolutions before being caught. It goes higher than a single spin. In order to give the club time for a high double spin it is necessary to throw it earlier so it is thrown from the left hand rather than the right one. It is thrown diagonally across to your partner's left hand.

So, in every other timing the club you catch from your partner in your left hand is immediately thrown back to him or her from the same hand as a double. It should arrive at exactly the same time and place as a regular throw.

Having thrown the double you have gained a little time and must resist the tendency to throw the next club that arrives in your right hand.

On every other timing the triple spin is thrown high up from the right hand immediately after you have made a regular pass.

It goes to your partner's left hand. After you have thrown the club you have a short while with one club in each hand and cannot throw the next pass until you have received a club from your partner and started to throw a club from your left to your right hand.

In the time that the triple is in the air and before you are passed a club from your partner you have time to turn a pirouette.

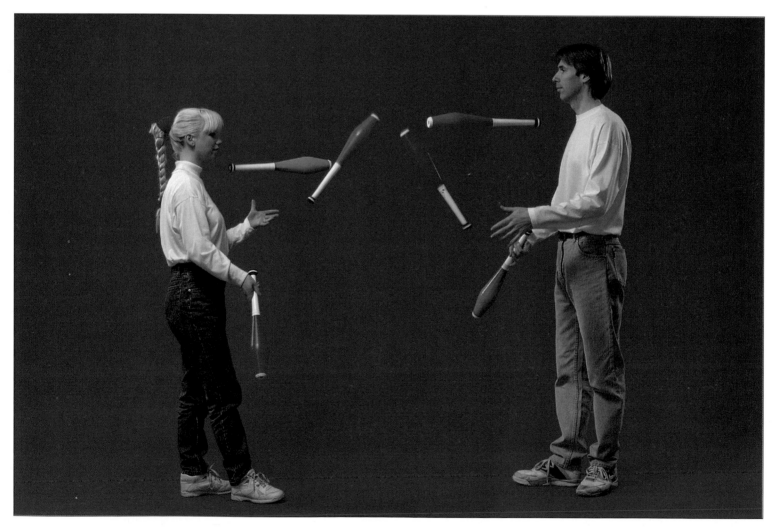

The clubs make one revolution as they are passed.

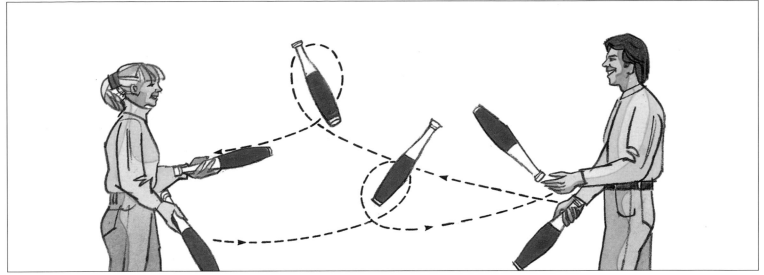

Each juggler here is passing single spins, throwing at the same time from the right to their partner's left hand.

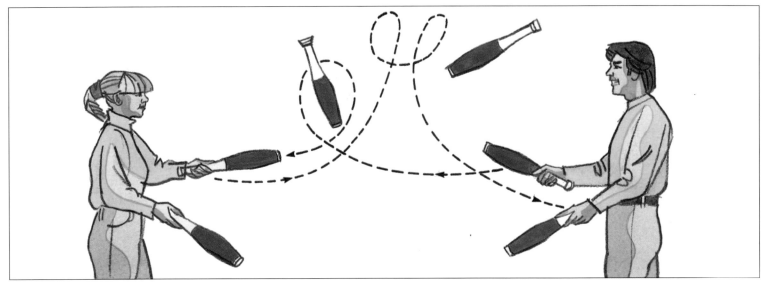

The juggler on the left throws the club she just caught as a double from her left hand to her partner's left hand.

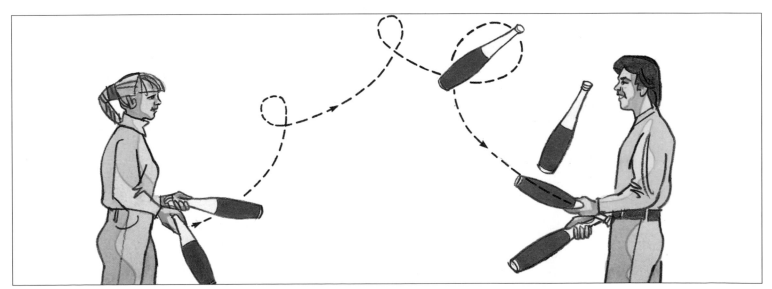

Having thrown a club from the right hand, the juggler on the left throws a triple from her right to her partner's left hand.

Under the Leg

If you can throw a club under a leg while juggling alone you can pass a club under the leg. You can either throw under your right leg from the outside or under your left leg from the inside. It helps to turn a little towards your right to ensure that the club goes wide of your partner.

The same applies to behind the back throws. Turn to your right, then throw the club from your right hand behind your back to your partner.

RIGHT
Katie prepared to bat the club across to Charlie.

Under the Leg

There are several possible variations on catching a club and batting it back. Throw a pass as usual but instead of carrying on juggling catch two clubs in your right hand and one in your left. You can either throw the club in your left hand across to your partner or you can bat it across with the two clubs in the right hand as shown in the photograph. The action is more of a push than a bat so that you retain control over the speed and direction of the club. Variations include pretending to do a tennis serve or, keeping hold of the handle, placing it top down on the ground and pretending to kick it up while really flicking it with up with your hand.

LEFT
You can throw under either leg to your partner.

Passing back to back is as difficult as it looks.

Back to Back

Stand back to back with your partner and throw the club up and straight back, not diagonally across the body.

It is very important to juggle and throw at the same time. Because you cannot see each other, when you raise your clubs to start it is a good idea to bang your clubs against your partner's clubs to signify starting and to count out loud. Practise on thirds and throw double spins.

Remember that your partner is just behind you so take care not to throw your club too far back. Keep talking to your partner giving advice on how accurate their throws are.

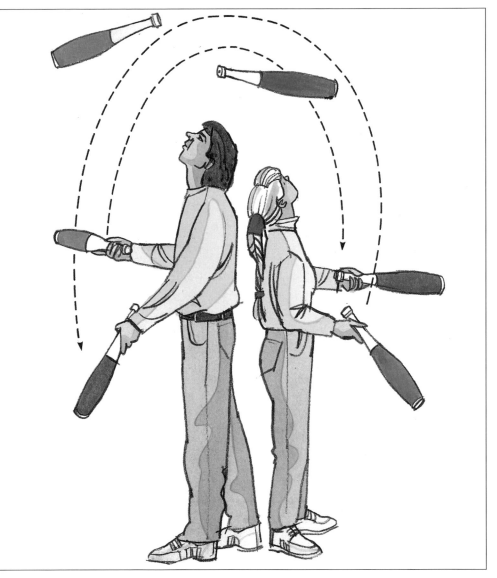

Juggle a normal Cascade, throw every third right-hand club over your right shoulder to your partner, who brings the left hand up ready to catch overhand. Your partner throws at the same time.

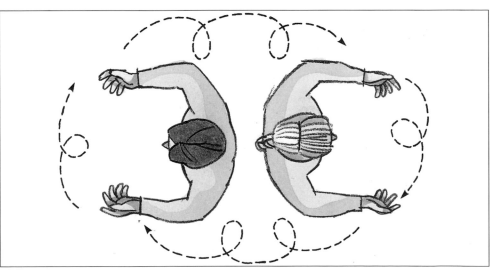

Back to back with double spins.

55

Multi-person Passing Patterns

Having learnt to pass with one other person you can move on to multi-person passing patterns.

The Feed

The Feed is the basic pattern. Here one juggler, the feeder, passes alternately to two (or more) other jugglers, the feedees. All three jugglers do a slow start at the same time with the feeder passing on every others first to the juggler to his right then to the juggler to his left. The feedees juggle on fourths (four, three, two, one, pass). To avoid passing at the same time as the other feedee, the feedee being thrown to second by the feeder must start on fourths rather than on thirds as usual with a slow start – counting four, three, two, one, pass – after which he continues to throw fourths.

You can then try having the feeder showering while the feedees throw every others. Try throwing double and triple spins as well.

The Triangle

Each juggler stands at the corner of an equilateral triangle and passes at the same time. A good way of measuring the distance is to stand with your arms and clubs outstretched so that they touch the end of the clubs held by the juggler on either side.

You can pass inside or outside. To pass inside you throw to the left hand of the person on your left. All three jugglers pass at the same time so it is important to throw accurately to the shoulder of the person you are throwing to. Turn and look at him or her when you throw, then turn to look at the club coming in from the other juggler.

If you are having problems check that you are each on the corner of an equidistant triangle and that you are juggling at the same tempo as each other.

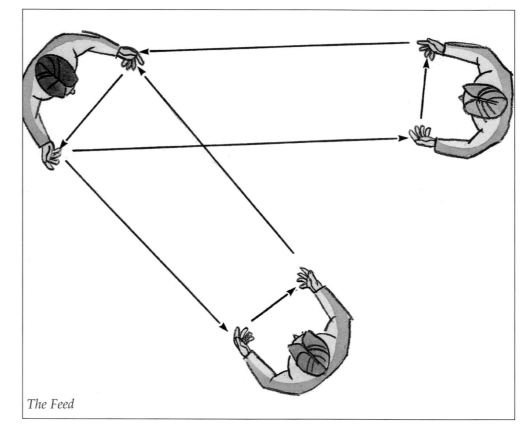

The Feed

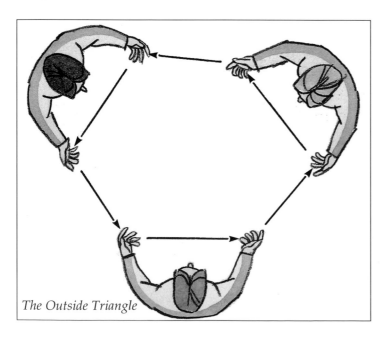

The Outside Triangle

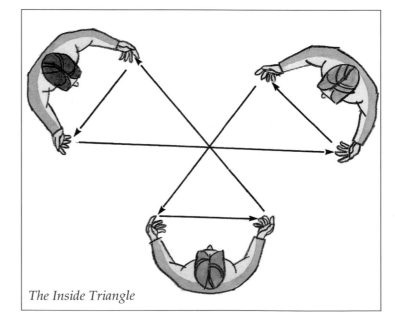

The Inside Triangle

To throw outside, throw to the left hand of the person on your right. Be aware that this is very close so it is necessary for you to throw a short, gentle pass

You can also do an inside, outside pattern where you alternately throw to the person on your left and the person on your right.

Learn the patterns on thirds then build up to every others and showering. You can also do a 3-3-10 and tricks.

The Box
This is one of the most exhilarating patterns when it works! Two jugglers pass clubs back and forth while another two jugglers are passing in the same zone.

Each juggler stands on the corner of a square and passes with the juggler diagonally opposite. To avoid collisions there is a staggered start with one pair of jugglers starting one count later than the other pair. One way of doing this is to start with two clubs in the left hand, so that there is an extra beat before the usual right hand throw in a slow start.

Try to build up from thirds to showering. It is also possible for all four to throw at the same time as long as you are accurately positioned on the corners of the square and pass and catch much wider than usual with your arms outspread. Watch out for flying clubs as there are bound to be collisions!

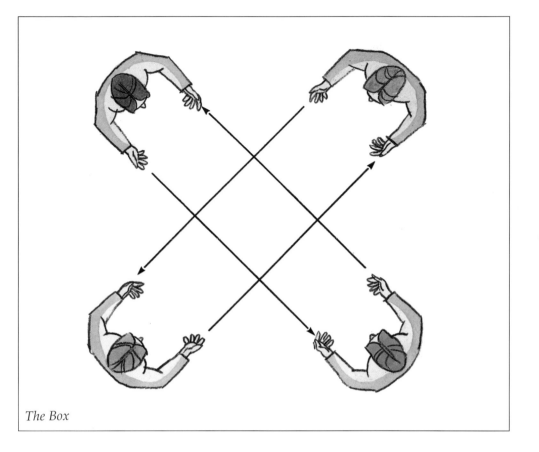

The Box

The Line
Three people can juggle in a line, two facing towards the third. Each starts with one club and begins to throw at the same time. The juggler on the left in the illustration below is throwing a short single spin to the juggler in the middle who is throwing a club back over the shoulder with a double spin to the juggler on the right. This juggler is throwing a long single spin pass to the first juggler. He or she should step

a bit to the right to avoid hitting the middle juggler.

The throw back over the shoulder is known as a drop back, so the middle juggler is dropping back.

The central juggler can stop juggling between passes and turn to face in the opposite direction. The juggler who was passing long now passes to the middle juggler and the juggler at the other end alters his or her juggling pattern to match.

The Line

CHAPTER SIX
THE DIABOLO, DEVIL STICKS, CIGAR BOXES AND PLATE SPINNING

There are many other areas of object manipulation related to juggling. In this chapter we provide an introduction to several of them.

The Diabolo

The diabolo is a relative of the yo-yo and spinning top. Chinese in origin and traditionally made from bamboo these egg-timer shape objects are now made from rubber. There are hundreds of tricks that can be done

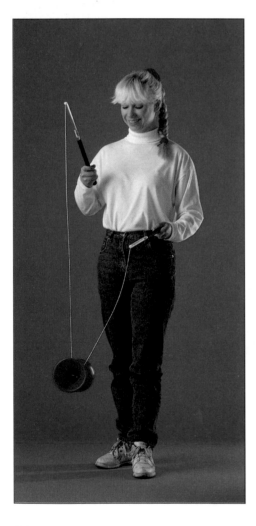

once you have learnt to get the diabolo spinning and under control.

Put the diabolo on the ground about a foot in front of you and a little to the side of your dominant hand and place the string underneath its waist. Hold the dominant hand-stick pointed down and raise the subordinate one to absorb the slack.

Raise the dominant hand to roll the diabolo along the ground then lift it off the ground. The diabolo will have gained a little anti-clockwise spin if you are right handed, or clockwise spin if you are left-handed.

It is crucial to keep the diabolo spinning the same way. To do this, as the diabolo reaches the end of the string drop the dominant hand-stick down so that the diabolo falls back to the start of the string and then vigorously scoop the stick up so that the diabolo is whipped up the string again. The dominant hand is doing the work, scooping and dropping, while the subordinate hand is mainly acting as a shock absorber, moving up and down a little but not whipping the diabolo along.

Once started, you must always be standing with the spindle at right-angles to you and an open bowl end of the diabolo towards you. If it starts to swing round you too must move around.

The diabolo may start to tilt backwards. To correct it pull your subordinate hand back and push your dominant hand forwards.

If the diabolo starts to tilt forward push your subordinate hand forwards and pull your dominant hand back.

Starting position for the Diabolo.

Raise the stick in the dominant hand to lift the Diabolo and give it spin.

If the Diabolo begins to tilt you must correct it.

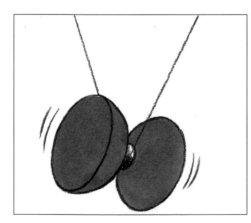

The Diabolo tilting back.

RIGHT
When you can spin the Diabolo you can catch it – sighting along the right hand stick to ensure that the Diabolo lands on the string.

Throwing and Catching the Diabolo

Before throwing the diabolo into the air it should be spinning fast, otherwise it is liable to tumble end over end, and be level, otherwise it will fly off in the direction it is leaning.

To throw the diabolo pull your arms apart to stretch the string taut and flick the diabolo up in the air. The more forceful the move the higher the diabolo will go.

Aim along your dominant hand-stick at the centre of the diabolo when it is high and catch the diabolo near the dominant handstick. Immediately lower your dominant hand to absorb the shock rather than allow the diabolo to bounce off the string. Start whipping the diabolo again to keep it spinning.

Climbing the String

Raise your subordinate hand up high so that the diabolo is spinning near the dominant hand. Loop the dominant hand-stick around the front of the diabolo and pull the string taut. If too taut the diabolo will jam, not taut

As the Diabolo lands, asorb the impact by dropping your right hand.

Throwing the Diabolo.

60

enough and it will not climb the string. Get it right and the diabolo will climb up the string as shown in the photograph right.

As it nears the top of the string unloop the diabolo by moving the subordinate hand stick down towards your face and up and over the diabolo.

Initiating the climb

Unlooping the Diabolo.

With the string wrapped around the waist of the Diabolo it can be made to climb the string.

61

The Impossible Knot just before it is untied.

The Impossible Knot

In this complex move a tangle is created and then swiftly released. It is best learnt, before trying it in action, with a friend holding the diabolo as it would be if it was spinning.

With the diabolo spinning take the dominant hand stick and move it outwards and round the end of the subordinate handstick, keeping the arms uncrossed, and pull the string back across the subordinate stick.

Carry the string over the subordinate stick then under the diabolo and between the subordinate stick and your body and then forward over the stick.

From this position bring the string

under the diabolo again and you will have formed an impossible knot.

To release the diabolo lower the front of the sticks so that the loops of string fall off and the diabolo will be

sitting on the string as it was at the beginning. Alternatively, point the sticks up and pull your arms apart releasing the loops from the sticks and throwing the diabolo into the air.

Beginning the Impossible Knot, the dominant stick brings the string across the subordinate one.

The string goes under the Diabolo and up on the inside of the subordinate stick.

The Diabolo in a knot.

The dominant hand stick goes over the subordinate under the Diabolo.

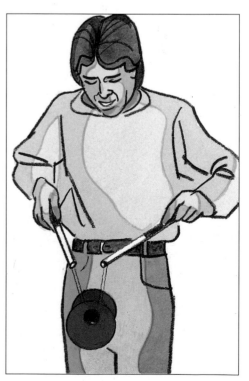

Releasing the Diabolo by pointing both sticks downwards.

The Diabolo held in the Cat's Cradle.

Cat's Cradle

This is another trick best tried first by performing all the motions while a friend holds the diabolo as though it were spinning. Follow the stages shown in the illustrations. When you think that you know them, start the diabolo and begin the real thing.

There are two ways to release the diabolo from the cradle. One way is to toss the diabolo gently into the air then pivot the tips of the sticks together and jerk them apart so that the string is released before catching the diabolo. Alternatively, point the tips of the sticks down to the ground and the loops of the cradle will fall off the sticks taking the diabolo down to the starting position.

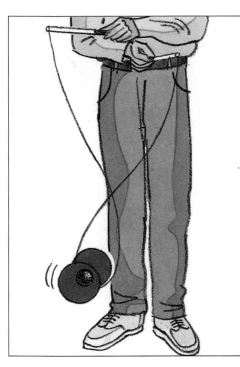

Swap the hand sticks over. Pass one to be held between thumb and index finger of the other hand then take the other stick as soon as the hand is free.

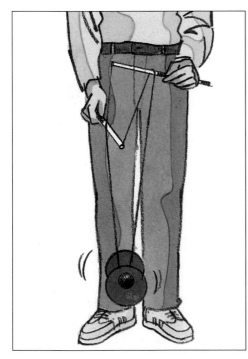

Put the end of the stick in the dominant hand through the triangle made by the stick and the string attached to it.

Take the subordinate hand stick and move it outwards and round the end of the dominant hand stick so that the strings are crossed.

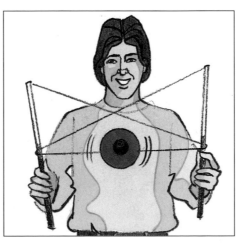

Point both sticks up in the air so that he Diabolo is now spinning on the lower string.

Carry the hand stick now in the dominant hand out and around the other stick so that the string hooks over the stick, keeping the arms uncrossed at all times.

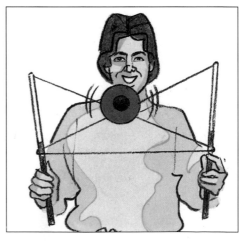

Push the Diabolo forwards and upwards into the air, then scoop the cradle underneath to catch it.

The Devil Stick

The devil stick defies the laws of gravity as it is spun around by the control sticks held in each hand.

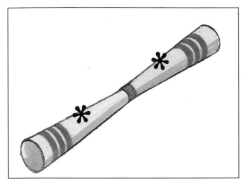

The devil stick should be struck at the points marked by the asterisks.

Contact points
The devil stick can defy gravity because it tapers towards the centre from each end so that when you hit it at one of the contact points, a quarter from the end, it gets a little lift. Your hand sticks should be parallel with each other and the ground, otherwise the devil stick will slide out of control. Rather than batting the devil stick back and forth you should be making more of a throw and catch action.

Getting the Devil Stick started
Kneel with the devil stick at an angle of about 45° with the upper contact point resting at the quarter

The starting position.

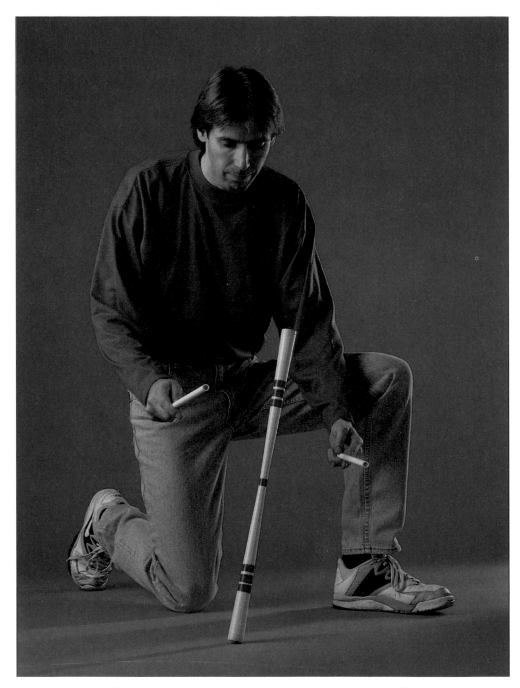

Knock the Devil Stick back and forth and try to stand up while controlling it with the hand sticks.

mark on a hand stick. Use the handstick to throw the devil stick until it rocks over and falls onto the other hand stick at an angle of about 45°. Repeat this back and forth, with the bottom end of the stick never leaving the ground. Gradually see if you can get the devil stick to lift a little off the ground by giving some upward push as well.

You can then carry it upwards until you can stand up to control it.

Starting in the air
Stand up and try the devil stick in the air. Balance the devil stick at the contact points on the hand sticks. Remove one of the hand sticks and as the devil stick starts to fall give it a push with the remaining hand stick so that it is thrown past vertical to an angle of 45° then catch it and throw it back with the other hand stick. Keep throwing it back and forth: concentrate on hitting the contact points.

The Propeller

This is an hard trick to learn, but one of the best. The devil stick seems to circle continuously around one hand stick just like a aeroplane propeller.

Throw the devil stick with the hand stick in the subordinate hand and, instead of knocking it back, with the dominant hand keep it spinning in the same direction by circling the devil stick with the hand stick and pushing it up just under the middle each time it comes around.

Starting in the air.

The Devil Stick is lifted by the subordinate hand just below its middle.

Tap the Devil Stick just below the middle of each revolution to keep it spinning around the one hand stick.

Plate Spinning

Plastic plates designed for spinning are available from juggling shops. These plates have a flange on the underside which makes working with them much easier. While not as inherently satisfying as china ones they are easier to spin and harder to break.

To begin, balance the inside of the flange on the underside of the plate on the point of the stick, which must be held absolutely vertical. Hold the stick right at the end. Make a gentle rotating action with your wrist so that the top of the stick starts to make small circles of about six inches (15cm) in diameter.

Gradually and smoothly increase the speed of the rotation and the plate will start to rise towards the horizontal. When it reaches horizontal and is spinning well stop your wrist action suddenly and the centre of the plate will jump to the point of the stick.

The plate will continue to spin for quite a while during which time you

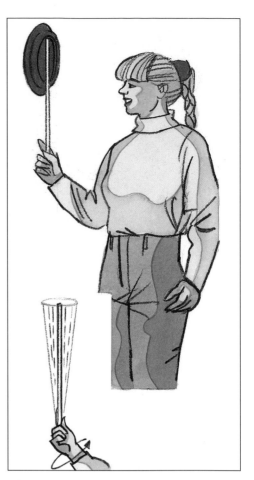

The starting position.

Keep the stick vertical to ensure the plate spins freely.

can do tricks. They are performed with the stick held vertical and without rotation.

Gently toss the plate up from the stick and catch it again.

Try balancing the stick and plate on your finger. See the club balance in chapter four for advice on balancing objects.

Try balancing the stick and plate on your chin. Be prepared to move your feet as well as your head to keep the balance. See how much you move your hand doing the trick above. Your head will need to move the same amount.

If you raise the top of your index finger to touch the plate next to the stick and at the same moment pull the stick away the plate will spin on it. You can then move your arm around and push the plate beneath it. It is much more difficult to increase rotation on a finger. As the speed drops use the stick again.

Tossing the plate.

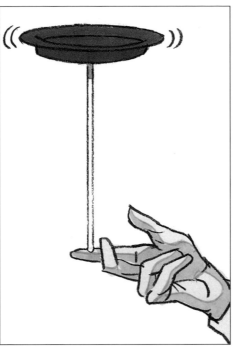

Finger balancing the stick.

Chin balancing the stick.

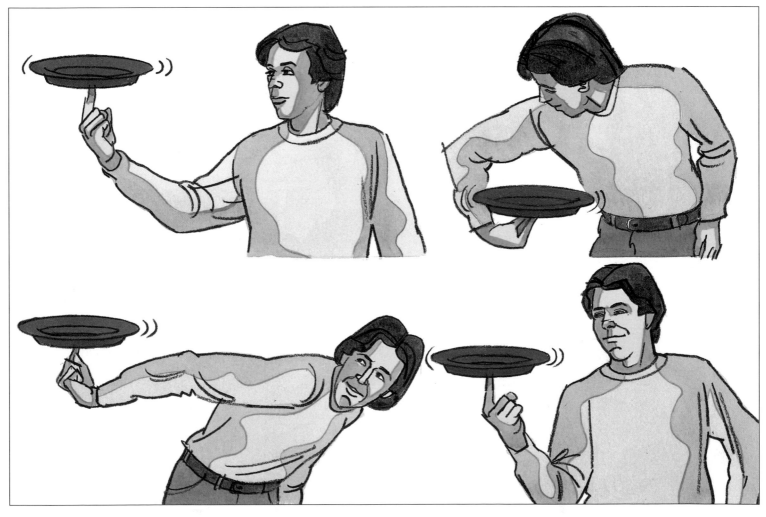

Replacing the stick with a forefinger and curling it under the arm.

Cigar Boxes

Real cigar boxes are rarely used for this trick. Juggling equipment suppliers sell sturdy, easy to grip boxes which are ideal for the novice.

Boxes in starting position.

Removing the end box.

Dropping to catch the centre box.

The right hand has grasped the box from the middle and is taking it right to the end.

Two boxes are held with a third pinned between them. The idea is to move the boxes around without letting the one, or ones, not being held fall to the ground. In effect the boxes you hold are used as extensions of the hand to catch those you release.

Hold the boxes at waist height, then raise your hands and pull one box away from the other two.

Lower your arms, bend at the knees and join the boxes up again.

Try the same move but pulling both end boxes away from the middle box and then catch it again.

The end turn.

End Turns

Raise your hands and pull one box away and turn your hand upside down so the box is turned through 180° and join the boxes up. To return to the starting position either reverse the move or release the end box with your hand, move your hand to on top of the box and grab it again.

Try turning both end boxes at the same time.

Take Outs

Take Outs are when you take out one of the boxes and shunt it along the pattern or change position so that a middle box becomes an end box.

Try almost the same trick as in End Turns but, instead of scooping the middle box down and around the end box, pull the middle box up and around the end box.

End Box Take Out

Here all three boxes are dropped together and one hand crosses to move one box to the opposite end. The middle box becomes the end box for the other end.

Raise the boxes, let go of the one of the outside boxes and grab the middle box.

Scoop it straight down and around the end box as shown above.

Trap the box you released initially in the centre.

Lift up and release all three boxes.

Grab one of the end boxes with the other hand from the one that was holding it.

Scoop it down and around to become the end box at the other end.

CHAPTER SEVEN
PERFORMING

Hat juggling by Las Piranhas from Germany.

Juggling can be viewed as an enjoyable sport, with the emphasis on working out and perfecting tricky new moves, or as a tool for use in performance.

The main strengths of juggling in performance are that it is hugely visual, has a natural rhythm to it, and that the constant risk of gravity getting the upper hand and the juggler dropping generates excitement and suspense. Plus relatively few people can juggle at all and very few can do several different tricks.

However if you go out to perform your juggling tricks on stage or in a shopping mall you will probably find

that juggling alone doesn't interest people for more than a few seconds.

Mentally your emphasis needs to be on creating an entertaining act which uses juggling. Unfortunately the fact that something is entertaining to do does not mean it is entertaining to watch and, secondly, the fact that it takes years of dedicated practice to master juggling seven balls does not guarantee it is entertaining either.

Juggling performances generally fall into one of two categories: the skill based routine and the comedy routine. Some advice on each of these follows. Try also to go and see what other performers are doing, both in juggling

and in related areas ranging from rhythmic gymnastics and dance to stand-up comedy.

Skill-based routines

Skill-based routines work best if they are devised to work with a carefully chosen piece of music. As you will be listening to it many times it is important that you enjoy the piece. Enjoying it also means that you will feel comfortable with it which will help you when you develop your performing character. Another thing to consider when choosing a piece of music is whether it will appeal to your audience and be appropriate to the type of venue in which you hope to be performing. If you don't know a lot about music, seeking out an expert to help you can save a lot of time and effort.

Most jugglers work to music that is purely instrumental or has very few lyrics as words can prove distracting. It helps if the music has a strong start and a distinct end rather than a fade out. One or two false ends in the piece are helpful as they provide natural pause and applause points.

As with any kind of performing you need an attention grabbing start, strong middle and spectacular end. Consider how you make your appearance on stage and choose a knock-out trick to start. This must be one you can do every time without fail. The same rule applies to the end trick.

List out the moves you can do reliably and work out ways of linking two or three moves together smoothly. Try to avoid coming back to the Cascade between tricks – although it is the easiest link it becomes repetitive. Practise these sequences while

listening to the music and experiment with varying the speed at which you juggle and the size of the pattern. Work on moves that will surprise an audience such as a seemingly accidentally dropped ball that bounces straight back into the pattern.

You should also experiment with moving while juggling. Some moves look very different from the side from how they look from the front. Try juggling while sitting down or kneeling as well as standing. To improve the calibre of your movement you can take up dance or gymnastic classes.

Consider also the props you are juggling, for example whether to use fat bodied or slim clubs to get the effect you want. You will also need to determine what costume to wear and what make up you need. You may like to seek out an expert in these areas from your local theatre group.

Bear in mind the type of background you will be working against. Beware of ending up juggling white balls while wearing a white shirt and standing against a white background!

The more ungainly you look the more amazed your audience will be at your skills.

Make use of mirrors, video cameras and friends to analyse what the routine you are creating looks like and how you can improve it. You may be able to find other jugglers interested in creating their own routines so that you can help each other to develop. Helping someone else is almost always a good way of helping yourself.

A Diabolo workshop on progress at a juggling convention in Leeds.

Comedy Routines

Comedy is a firm favourite with audiences and there are classic tricks which take advantage of the potential for comic tension.

One example is juggling an apple, an onion and an egg with the intention of eating the apple while juggling. The audience is intrigued to know whether you can eat while juggling, and whether you can choose which object to eat. They will also find it very hard to resist waiting to see what happens if you bite the onion or the egg – and will empathise with the horrified expression on your face as you make the mistake!

There are many tricks such as the one above that are considered to be in the public domain and therefore permissable for anyone to use. The risk with them is that audiences may have been overexposed to them. Novelty is important to an audience. For this reason try to come up with your own fresh ideas. If you see someone doing a great and original trick resist the temptation to steal it, just as you hope that others won't steal your original material. Do use their example to spur your own imagination and see if you can come up with something wilder or wackier.

Audiences like surprises and it is always worthwhile finding different and improbable objects to juggle rather than using objects made for juggling. A briefcase, umbrella and mobile phone being juggled is bound to attract attention – particularly if the phone rings half-way through the routine!

Risk is another audience pleaser. Juggling glass bottles carries inherent risk of breakage, increased as the

'Eating The Apple' – without eating the onion or the egg.

A five ball endurance competition at a european juggling convention in Germany.

74

juggler realises that he has to catch two bottles in one hand to end – or can he find a way out?

If you use regular juggling objects can they seem to have a mind of their own, or can you do impressions (such as the Yo-Yo or the Penguin)? Try to work out moves that conjure up images of objects or actions, or that just look plain idiotic!

As you start to think about possible material think also about your stage character. The character in which you feel comfortable performing is almost always based on your own character and opinions. An audience can tell at once if you are uncomfortable with the character you are portraying. Work on developing your character just as you work on

your juggling. Think about the clothes, music, movement and voice of the character and gradually exaggerate them sufficiently to become noticeable as a stage character.

Consider taking acting or clown classes to improve your performing technique.

The Long and the Short of It – author Charlie Holland with his partner Olly Crick ready for their Breton Brother's restaurant juggling routine.

Juggling has a history dating back at least 4,000 years. The earliest known paintings of juggers found in the tombs of ancient Egypt were made around 2,000 BC and there are many representations of jugglers in Greek art from around 400 BC. A wonderful statue made of baked clay was found at Thebes. It dates from 200 BC and shows a juggler with a ball balanced

Juggling has a history dating back at least 4,000 years. The earliest known paintings of jugglers found in the tombs of ancient Egypt were made around 2,000 BC and there are many representations of jugglers in Greek art from around 400 BC. A wonderful statue made of baked clay was found at Thebes. It dates from 200 BC and shows a juggler with a ball balanced

the word juggler today. An illustration from the mid-1700s shows a French juggler and rope-walker, Mathieu Dupuis, juggling three apples and catching them on three forks, one held in each hand and one in the mouth.

From around the beginning of the nineteenth century juggling became a staple part of the emerging

A postcard portrait of diabolo performer Miss Coralie Blythe.

A popular postcard of the early 1900's.

entertainment forms: circus, variety and vaudeville.

Juggling acts from the Orient became popular introducing such objects as the devil-stick and mouthsticks for balancing balls on. Another juggling implement introduced from the East was the diabolo, which came from China and was originally made from bamboo.

In the early 1900s playing with the diabolo became a craze that happened to coincide with another new craze, sending postcards. Hundreds of different cards, such as the ones shown here, were produced with subjects including children and famous actors and actresses of the day.

Enrico Rastelli, the juggler often considered as the greatest of all time, was inspired by the work of a Japanese juggler Takashima. Born in 1897 into a juggling family, Rastelli broke the records for numbers of objects juggled. He could juggle ten small balls or eight plates. However he was best known for his amazingly skillful manipulation and balancing of leather footballs. He died tragically young in 1931 as a result of a cut from his mouthstick to his gum which became infected. So popular was he that thousands of mourners attended his funeral.

Another great juggler in the early twentieth century was Paul Cinquevalli who became known as the 'The Human Billiard Table' for his most famous routine in which he juggled and rolled balls around his body and caught them in special pockets on his green felt jacket. For the finale of his act he caught a 48lb cannonball on the back of his neck.

Cinquevalli's original tricks led him to become the inspiration for a new genre of juggling, the 'Gentlemen Jugglers', who juggled such everyday items as billiard balls, hats, cigars, walking sticks, crockery and chairs! The appeal of being able to exercise such control over everyday objects continues today with jugglers such as Steve Rawlings who balances wine bottles and juggles furniture.

Other themes were adopted – a common one being a restaurant setting

Paul Cinquevalli with his cannonball

on stage with a troupe of jugglers acting as customers and waiters. There is a fine film of American juggler Bobby May borrowing a cigar off a snowman to manipulate with his hat and gloves. He is pelted with snowballs by local children and catches them all under his hat, then proceeds to bounce juggle these astounding rubber snowballs!

W.C. Fields, who was to become known as one of the funniest film comedians, had an early career as 'The Eccentric Tramp Juggler' He described some of his tricks with hats and cigars, and manipulating cigar boxes in A *Magician's Handbook* published in 1904.

The Kremo family from Switzerland are one of the most enduring juggling dynasties. Kris Kremo juggles balls, hats and cigar boxes, including a triple pirouette with the latter.

There were several books devoted to juggling technique in the early twentieth century such as *The Art of Modern Juggling* by Anglo and *Juggling or How to Become a Juggler* by Rupert Ingalese. Ingalese's book included a mail order catalogue in the back with Imitation Juggling Umbrellas, the Great Comedy Cannon Ball Trick and Juggling Clubs at 55 shillings for three a costly purchase at that time. The clubs are described as follows:

Top comedy juggler Steve Rawlings with fire torches.

"The finest in the world. These clubs are covered with fine quality canvas, have hardwood handles and are practically unbreakable. They are beautifully decorated, ready for professional use, and are very light, the weight being only about 16 ounces. They are 21 inches long, and are identical with those used by all the leading Club Jugglers."

Other clubs had wooden dowels with a basket of bamboo strips to give the bulbous shape. Fibreglass clubs were introduced by Stu Reynolds and these in turn led onto the moulded plastic club of today.

Club juggling and passing evolved at the turn of the century and many of the tricks done today date from these early days.

For supreme numbers juggling it is usual to look to Russia where the circus schools produced jugglers such as Ignatov who juggled eleven rings.

Dance has been incorporated with juggling by several jugglers who recognise the potential for integrating the movement of the body with the movement of the objects. Francis Brunn's use of Flamenco dance gave his act sensational poise, elegance and precision. One of the most popular troupes to emerge in the 1980s was Airjazz, comprising Jon Held, Peter Davidson and Kezia Tenenbaum, whose sophisticated use of music and contemporary dance alongside their strong juggling skills made their routines exceptionally rhythmical. More recently the Gandini Juggling Project has gone further into merging contemporary dance with juggling to the point where juggling is incorporated in the dancing rather than the other way round.

One of the most respected of today's jugglers is Michael Moschen whose fluid rolling of crystal balls from the front to the back of his hands and around his body has inspired a whole contact juggling movement.

He has also created a bounce juggling routine inside a triangle using the sound of the bounces at different times to create juggling music.

Creating juggling music is a hallmark of The Flying Karamazov Brothers who formed in the 1970s in California and have been touring ever since, often with The Grateful Dead. They created back drums – electronic drum pads which they carry on their backs so that they can hit them with their clubs as they juggle. Noise of another nature is a part of their show too – as they throw chain saws at each other! Not a trick to imitate!

There are now more jugglers than ever before. New tricks are being invented and old ones rediscovered. I hope that the next 4,000 years of juggling will prove as interesting as the past.

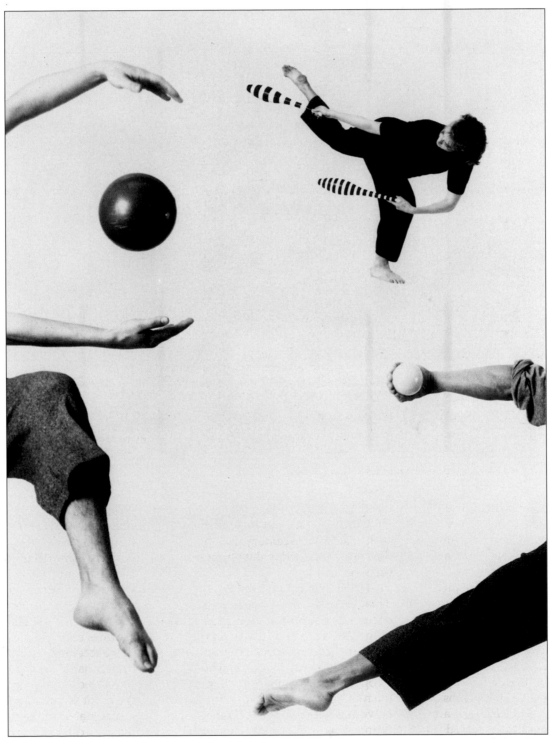

The Gandini Juggling Project, merging contemporary dance with juggling.

WHERE TO GO FOR FURTHER INFORMATION ON JUGGLING

There are three main specialist juggling magazines: *Jugglers' World* published in America, *Kaskade* published in Germany with an English edition also, and *The Catch,* published in Britain. These carry articles on performers, reviews of shows, advertisements for shops and courses, advice on learning tricks and, most importantly, details of juggling groups and conventions!

There are now juggling groups meeting regularly in most cities and many small towns. As you would expect, the jugglers come together to swap tricks and throw objects at each other. It is easy to be intimidated on your first visit to a meeting by the awesome skills on display. Expert jugglers are normally willing to spend time helping a beginner. Remember that they were once beginners themselves.

As well as these small meetings there are regular juggling conventions. Forget images of dull meetings in lecture halls. The phrase 'juggling convention' is a misnomer for 'juggling jamboree' with masses of space for masses of jugglers to juggle and equipment retailers to show off their newest products. There are workshops in all sorts of skills and shows featuring all sorts of performers.

The big conventions are the International Jugglers' Association annual gathering in America which attracts about one thousand jugglers and the annual European Juggling Convention which attracts around two thousand. Alongside these are many smaller conventions which often provide a better chance to get to know other jugglers than the hustle and bustle of the big ones.

The best source of information about upcoming conventions is the juggling magazines and their addresses are:

Jugglers' World
International Jugglers' Association
P.O. Box 218
Montague
MA 01351
USA

Kaskade
Annastrasse 7
D-65197 Wiesbaden
Germany

The Catch
Moorledge Farm Cottage
Knowle Hill
Chew Magna
Bristol BS16 8TL
England